S0-BYX-463

# Lobsters

## and Other Crustaceans

Book Author: Christina Johnson
**For World Book:**
Editorial: Paul A. Kobasa, Scott Thomas, Christine Sullivan
Research: Cheryl Graham
Graphics and Design: Sandra Dyrlund, Brenda Tropinski
Photos: Tom Evans
Permissions: Janet Peterson
Indexing: David Pofelski
Proofreading: Tina Ramirez
Pre-press and Manufacturing: Carma Fazio, Anne Fritzinger, Steve Hueppchen

**For information about other World Book publications, visit our Web site at http://www.worldbookonline.com or call 1-800-WORLDBK (967-5325). For information about sales to schools and libraries, call 1-800-975-3250 (United States); 1-800-837-5365 (Canada).**

World Book, Inc.
233 N. Michigan Avenue
Chicago, IL 60601
U.S.A.

**The Library of Congress has cataloged an earlier edition of this title as follows:**

Lobsters and other crustaceans.
    p. cm. -- (World Book's animals of the world)
    Includes bibliographical references and index.
    ISBN 0-7166-1270-4
    1. Lobsters--Juvenile literature. 2. Crustacea--
Juvenile literature. I. World Book, Inc. II. Series.
QL444.M33L63 2005
595.3'84--dc22
                                    2004016491

**This edition:**
Lobsters: ISBN-10: 0-7166-1336-0  ISBN-13: 978-0-7166-1336-7
Set 4: ISBN-10: 0-7166-1285-2      ISBN-13: 978-0-7166-1285-8

Printed in Malaysia
3 4 5 6 7 8 09 08 07

**Picture Acknowledgments:** Cover: © Jen & Des Bartlett, Bruce Coleman Inc.; © Kike Calvo, Bruce Coleman Inc.; © Herb Segars, Animals Animals; © Mike Severns, Tom Stack & Associates; © Tom & Therisa Stack, Tom Stack & Associates.

© Thomas Aichinger, V&W/SeaPics.com 4, 39; © Jelle Atema 21; © Jen & Des Bartlett, Bruce Coleman Inc. 57; © Tom Branch, Photo Researchers 59; © Kike Calvo, Bruce Coleman Inc. 51; © Bob Cranston, Animals Animals 9; © E. R. Degginger, Bruce Coleman Inc. 47; © E. R. Degginger, Photo Researchers 5, 11; © Jack Dermid, Bruce Coleman Inc. 49; © Dave B. Fleetham, Tom Stack & Associates 23; © Michele Hall, SeaPics.com 17; © Richard Herrmann, SeaPics.com 35; © Breck P. Kent, Animals Animals 29; © George D. Lepp, Photo Researchers 31; © Scott Leslie, SeaPics.com 19; © Zig Leszczynski, Animals Animals 25; © Andrew J. Martinez, Photo Researchers 3, 7; © Flip Nicklin, Minden Pictures 37; © Doug Perrine, SeaPics.com 33; © Fritz Prenzel, Animals Animals 9; © James P. Rowan 43; © G. Van Ryckevorsel, Getty Images 61; © Herb Segars, Animals Animals 9; © Mike Severns, Tom Stack & Associates 9; © John Shaw, Bruce Coleman Inc. 41; © Scott W. Smith, Animals Animals 27; © Tom & Therisa Stack, Tom Stack & Associates 53; © Jeremy Stafford-Deitsch, SeaPics.com 5, 55; © Rainer Voigt 21; © M.I. Walker, Science Source/Photo Researchers 45.

**Illustrations:** WORLD BOOK illustrations by John Fleck 13, 15.

# World Book's Animals of the World

# Lobsters
## and Other Crustaceans

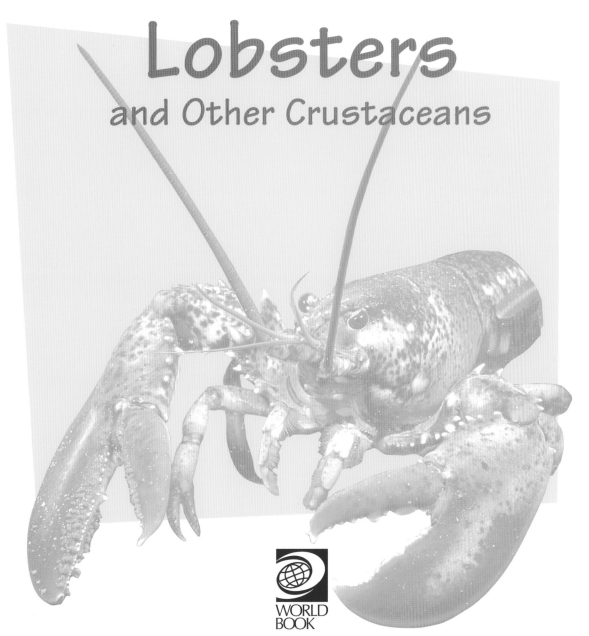

WORLD BOOK

a Scott Fetzer company
Chicago
www.worldbookonline.com

# Contents

You may think
I'm a lobster,
but I'm not!

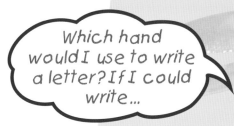

Which hand would I use to write a letter? If I could write...

Do you like fiddle music? Can I play you a tune?

# What Is a Crustacean?

Crustaceans *(kruhs TAY shuhnz)* are animals that have many jointed legs and a hard external shell. They are invertebrates, which means they do not have internal bones, not even a backbone. Instead, their outer shell, called an exoskeleton *(EHK soh SKEHL uh tuhn),* covers and protects their body.

Lobsters are a type of crustacean, and there are several types of lobster. American, or northern, lobsters are clawed lobsters. They are the largest kind of lobster. At full size, an American lobster can reach 42 inches (107 centimeters) in length and can weigh nearly 45 pounds (20 kilograms). Most American lobsters harvested today, however, are only about 8 inches (20 centimeters) long and weigh only about a pound (0.45 kilogram).

Two other types of lobsters, spiny and slipper lobsters, are clawless.

Crabs, crayfish, and shrimp are crustaceans, too. So are barnacles and wood lice.

American lobster

# Where in the World Do Lobsters and Other Crustaceans Live?

Lobsters and other crustaceans inhabit all the world's major oceans. Although lobsters can be found worldwide, different types of lobster choose different areas in which to live. Many lobsters live in shallow water in the coastal areas around islands. One group of lobsters, called deep-sea lobsters, lives in the cold, deep sea.

American lobsters thrive in the cool waters of the North Atlantic Ocean. These lobsters inhabit sandy, muddy, and rocky areas of the ocean floor from Virginia in the United States to Newfoundland and Labrador in Canada.

Spiny and slipper lobsters are found in warm waters throughout the world. Spiny lobsters live in coral reefs, on rock ledges, and in crevices. Slipper lobsters are usually found in muddy or sandy places.

8

# How Can You Tell It's a Lobster?

If you see an animal walking on the sea floor, and it has a jointed tail, two long antennae, two short antennae, lots of legs, and dark eyes that are on stalks, it is likely to be a lobster.

You can count the number of segments in its tail. A lobster's tail is made of seven distinct pieces, including the fanlike tip.

Another way to identify a lobster is by the number of its legs. Lobsters have five pairs of legs. Clawed lobsters, such as the American lobster, have front legs that end in large claws. The next two sets of legs have smaller pincers on their tips. Both clawed and clawless lobsters have delicate, leglike limbs under their abdomen that are used for swimming. These limbs are called swimmerets.

Lobsters are known as decapods. "Deca" is a Greek word that means 10, and "pod" is a Greek word that means foot. In addition to the lobster, other 10-footed crustaceans include shrimp and crayfish.

American lobster

11

# How Are Lobsters Like Knights in Armor?

In days of old, knights wore suits of armor to protect themselves in battle. Lobsters have a natural protective shell of their own, made of a material called chitin *(KY tihn)*.

Like a suit of armor, a lobster's exoskeleton is made of not one, but many, solid pieces. Some of the pieces are permanently attached to one another and do not move. Others are connected by a flexible material, which lets a lobster move freely.

The exoskeleton of an American lobster is made of 21 different pieces. The head has 6 pieces, the thorax (middle part) 8 pieces, and the tail, 7 pieces. The thickest part of a lobster's shell—on its back—is called the carapace *(KAR uh pays)*. You can think of it as a shield.

Because lobsters are invertebrates, their shell is their body's only structural support. A lobster's muscles are attached to its outer skeleton (shell) as ours are to our internal skeleton. Without its shell, a lobster could not move.

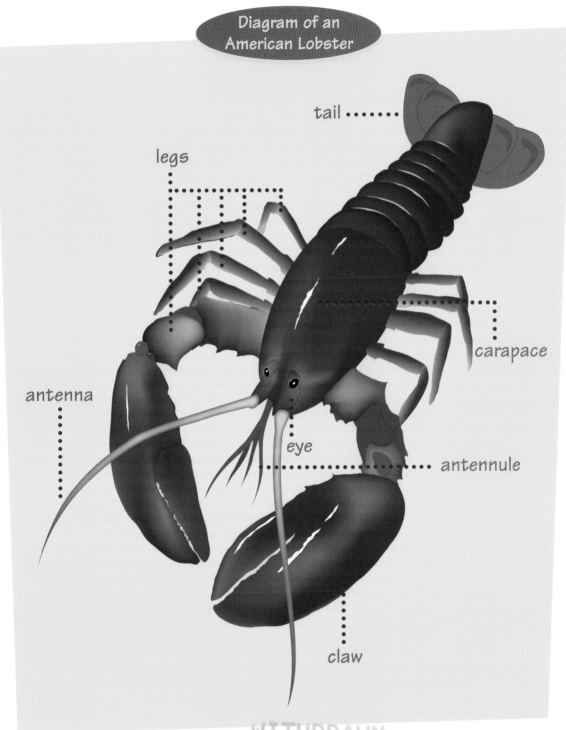

Diagram of an American Lobster

tail ·······

legs

carapace

antenna

eye

antennule

claw

# Are Lobsters Hollow?

Lobsters look like they might be hollow, but that is not the case.

Lobsters have the same major internal body structures as humans. Lobsters have a heart that pumps blood around its body and a brain that connects to a nervous system. For eating, digesting, and eliminating food, the lobster has a mouth, stomach, intestines, and anus. Lobsters also have sex organs for reproducing.

While lobsters share similarities with vertebrates, they are much more similar in structure to other invertebrates, especially insects. Like insects, lobsters have an open circulatory system. Animals with such a system lack blood vessels in some areas of their bodies. Blood flows directly into these areas and delivers oxygen and nutrients to the organs and tissues.

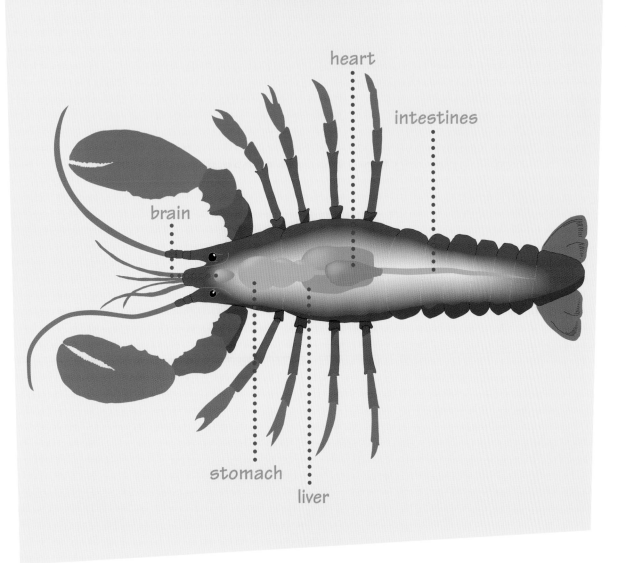

An American Lobster's
Internal Organs

heart

intestines

brain

stomach

liver

# What Is Molting?

It is hard for lobsters to grow. A lobster is, in a sense, trapped in its exoskeleton, because its shell cannot grow larger. For its body to grow larger, a lobster must discard its shell and replace it with a bigger one. This process is called molting.

Before a lobster molts, it forms a new, soft exoskeleton underneath its existing shell. When the lobster is ready to molt, it seeks out a protected place; it is vulnerable to attack until its new shell hardens.

To molt, the lobster shrinks the muscles and other tissues in its limbs by releasing fluid out of the tissues. This lets the lobster withdraw its appendages from the surrounding shell. Once the shell cracks, the lobster is able to withdraw its entire body from its old shell.

After it is out of its shell, the lobster takes in water to swell its body to a larger size. The new soft shell can withstand the pressure from the lobster's swollen body without cracking. It takes several weeks for the new shell to harden around the swollen lobster. Once the new shell is hard, the lobster pushes the excess water out from its body. It now has a new, roomier shell to grow into.

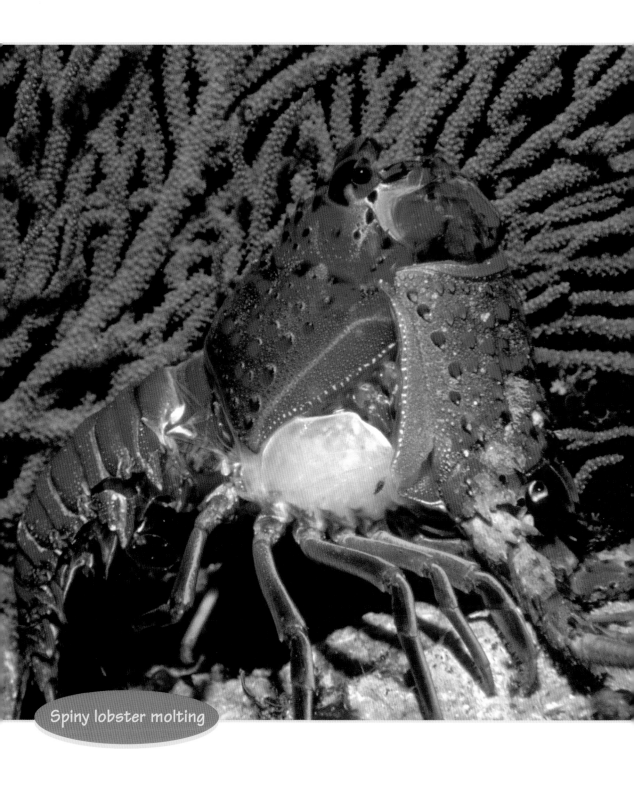

Spiny lobster molting

# Can All Lobsters See?

Some lobsters cannot see at all. Deep-sea lobsters, which live in deep and dark places in the ocean, are completely blind. Other lobsters, however, have two working eyes that sit on top of short, movable stalks. Under a microscope, you can see that a lobster's eyes have anywhere from dozens to thousands of tiny lenses. Eyes like these are called compound eyes.

Imagine a dome covered in tiles. This is what the surface of a compound eye looks like. Each tile is a lens. If you could count all the tiles, you'd find that some kinds of lobsters can have as many as about 10,000 lenses.

Compound eyes are good at detecting motion. They are also good at gathering light under dim conditions. This is important, because lobsters live underwater, where it can be dark.

Eyes of an
American lobster

# How Does a Lobster Taste, Hear, and Feel Its World?

A lobster does not smell with a nose, taste with a tongue, or hear with ears. Instead, the animal has special sense organs for collecting information about its marine environment.

Much of the information a lobster gets about its surroundings is gathered by millions of tiny hairlike sensors on its antennae, mouthparts, legs, and shell. Some of these sensors "sniff" chemicals that help lobsters locate and taste food. Others warn lobsters of predators or alert them to potential mates.

A lobster also has special organs located at the base of its antennules, as the shorter pair of antennae are called. These organs are pits that are lined with tiny bristles. As a lobster moves, particles that are floating within the pits bend the tiny bristles in different directions. Signals that are sent from these bristles through the lobster's nervous system help the lobster determine its position in its surroundings and keep its balance.

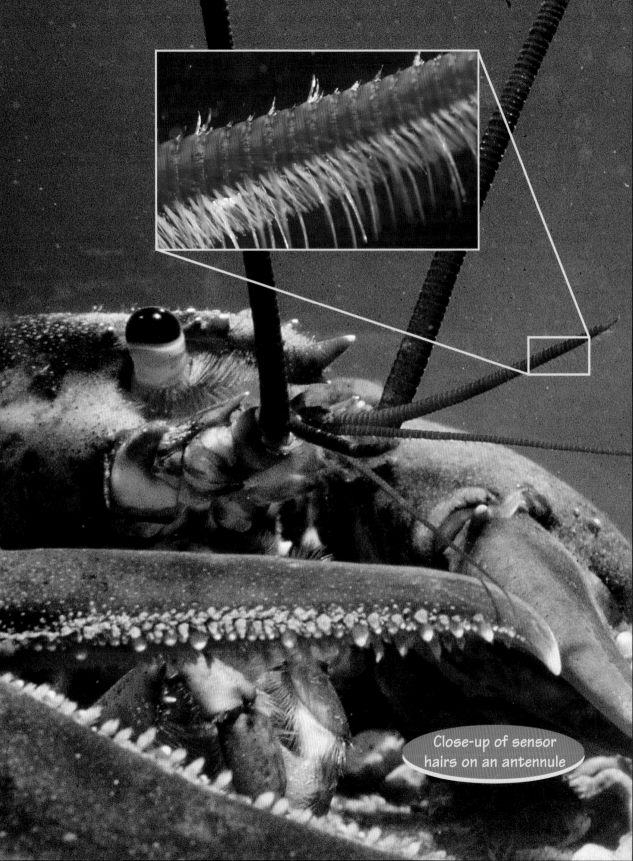

Close-up of sensor
hairs on an antennule

# Where Are a Lobster's Gills?

A lobster has gills at the base of its walking legs. Can you imagine breathing from your hips?

Gills are feathery, blood-filled organs that extract oxygen from seawater. The blood from the gills travels to other parts of the lobster's body, delivering oxygen along the way. Our lungs and circulatory system perform a similar task. A lobster must keep water moving across its gills—in the same way that humans must keep breathing—to maintain a steady supply of oxygen.

Not all crustaceans, however, have gills. Very small crustaceans with very thin "crusts" absorb oxygen directly through their shell. And, some land-living crabs breathe air with lungs instead of using gills to absorb oxygen from water.

Spiny lobster

# What Do Lobsters Eat?

Lobsters are not finicky eaters. They eat animals, such as fish or shellfish, as well as plants. Crowded into a tank, they may even snack on each other.

American lobsters are capable of catching small fish with their claws. They also hunt snails, sea urchins, and clams, crushing them with their claws.

Besides hunting live prey, lobsters scavenge the sea floor for dead and rotting animal carcasses, also known as carrion. Deep-sea lobsters, in fact, feed on the carcasses of whales, fish, and other dead animals. On land, large birds called vultures break down and recycle the nutrients of the dead creatures they eat. In the ocean, lobsters play this important role in recycling the sea's nutrients.

Lobster eating
a herring

# Are Lobsters "Left-handed" or "Right-handed"?

If you look closely at a lobster, you can see that one of its claws is larger than the other. The larger, heavier claw has thick teeth for crushing prey. The smaller claw is like a steak knife. It has sharp teeth the lobster uses to seize and slice its food.

Not all lobsters have the larger claw on the same side. A lobster is "left-handed" or "right-handed" depending on which side has the larger claw.

Do you think the lobster shown in the picture at right is left-handed or right-handed?

Claws of an
American lobster

# How Many Brothers and Sisters Does an American Lobster Have?

A newly hatched American lobster has thousands of brothers and sisters. A female lobster can lay nearly 100,000 eggs at a time! Can you imagine having 100,000 brothers and sisters?

Unlike many other animals that lay eggs, a female American lobster does not deposit her eggs in a nest. She carries her eggs, holding them under her body attached to her swimmerets for 10 or 11 months. A sticky substance covering the eggs glues them together. When the eggs are ready to hatch, a female shakes her swimmerets, opening the tiny eggshells.

As a general rule, animals that reproduce in such large numbers do so because most of their offspring die young. Life is very dangerous for young lobsters. All sorts of fish, octopuses, and sea birds feed on young lobsters. So, although a lobster may begin life with many brothers and sisters, by the time it is an adult, most of them will have perished.

Female American
lobster with eggs

# What Happens After a Lobster Hatches?

A newly hatched lobster looks like a see-through flea with huge black eyes. It is not a miniature version of an adult lobster. It first goes through a free-swimming stage. It is known as a larva *(LAHR vuh)* in that stage, and it is about ⅓ of an inch (0.8 centimeter) long. A larval lobster has a soft body and delicate, featherlike limbs. It propels itself by moving these limbs in a rapid rowing motion.

A newborn lobster spends its first two or three weeks of life swimming at the surface, feeding on tiny floating organisms.

During this time, it molts often. Each time it molts, the lobster becomes more like an adult lobster, growing a hard shell, jointed legs, and long antennae. By the time a lobster settles on the sea floor, it is ready to begin its life as a bottom-dweller.

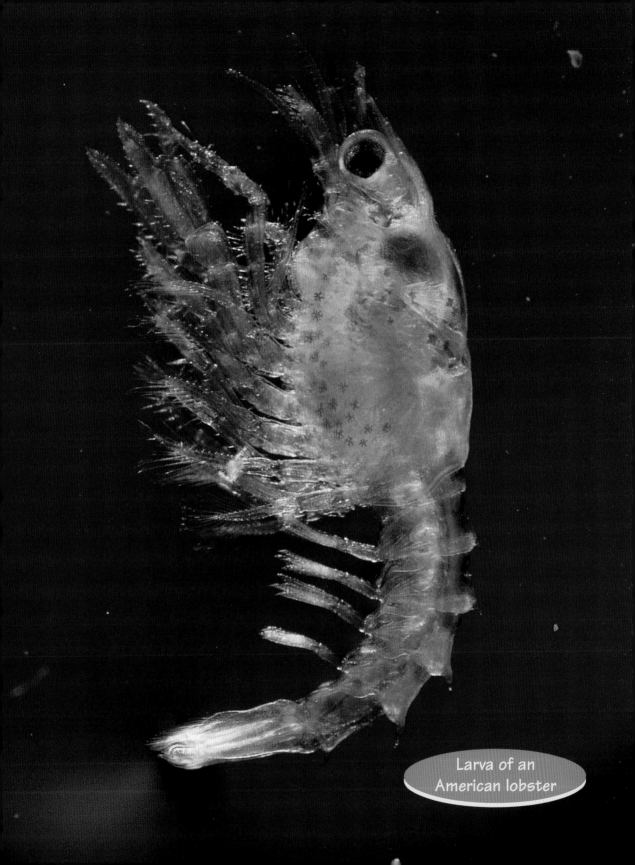

Larva of an
American lobster

# What Is a Lobster March?

To protect themselves from predators, fish swim in schools. Birds fly in flocks. And lobsters "march." Predators often have a difficult time capturing prey traveling in such groups.

During a lobster march, dozens of spiny lobsters walk together in long rows, like ants or soldiers. The lobsters walk so close together that the antennae of one lobster may touch the tail of the lobster in front of it.

In the Caribbean Sea, lobster marches are often observed after a storm. At these times, the lobsters are usually marching out to deeper water. Some people believe that storms trigger lobster marches. Scientists, however, are not sure why spiny lobsters march to other locations. Are they moving to deeper waters to protect themselves from winter storms? Are they looking for new breeding grounds? New feeding grounds? The answer remains a mystery.

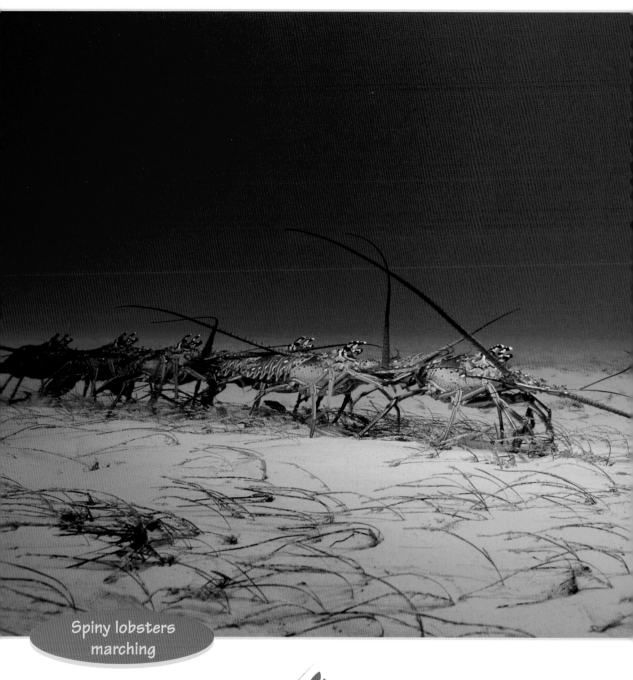

Spiny lobsters
marching

33

# How Do Lobsters Evade Predators?

Although an American lobster's claws are formidable weapons, lobsters are shy and try to avoid conflict. Still, claws are often a necessary defense against a hungry octopus or codfish.

Another defense many kinds of lobster have is the ability to lose a limb. Lobsters and many other crustaceans can voluntarily detach a limb that has been grabbed by a predator. When a lobster loses a limb, it can sometimes grow another in a process called regeneration.

Spiny lobsters have developed a unique and interesting defense. Octopuses like to eat spiny lobsters. Moray eels like to eat octopuses. So, spiny lobsters sometimes share a den with a moray eel. If an octopus tries to prey upon a spiny lobster, its "bodyguard," the eel, attacks and eats the octopus.

Both the spiny lobster and the moray eel benefit from being "roommates."

34

Moray eel (top) and spiny lobster (below)

35

# Which Crustaceans Are Seafood?

Many types of crustacean are edible, or fit to be eaten. People in kitchens all over the world take advantage of this.

Throughout the world, the crustaceans most popular as seafood are shrimp, crabs, and lobsters. In addition to these animals, other crustaceans are prized as food in specific regions. For instance, barnacles are a delicacy in parts of Europe and South America. Crayfish are a centerpiece of spicy Creole and Cajun cuisines of Louisiana.

Ecologically, crustaceans are an important source of food for marine animals of all sizes and shapes. Tiny crustaceans called copepods are food for small fish. Krill are the main source of nutrients for many whales and penguins. Because they are so rich in nutrients, krill also have been thought of as a potential source of food for people.

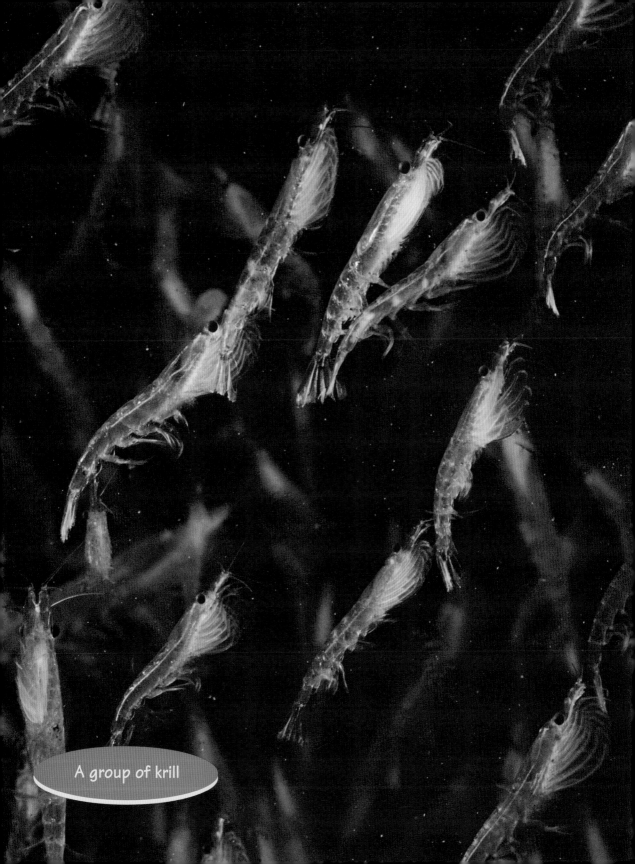

A group of krill

# What Are the Differences Between a Lobster and a Crayfish?

Clawed lobsters and crayfish are very similar. They have the same body structure: the same number of legs, the same number of antennae, a long tail, two claws, and a hard outer shell. Both also have two compound eyes. In fact, crayfish look more like clawed lobsters than do spiny lobsters.

There are, however, two important differences between clawed lobsters and crayfish. The first is size. Adult crayfish are usually 2 to 6 inches (5 to 15 centimeters) long. Commercially sold American lobsters are usually about 8 inches (20 centimeters) long and can grow much longer if left unharvested in the sea.

The second major difference is where crayfish live. Lobsters live in the ocean. Crayfish inhabit lakes, streams, and rivers. Crayfish are common in North America, Asia, Australia, and Europe.

A stone crayfish

39

# What Are the Differences Between a Shrimp and a Lobster?

As their name suggests, shrimp are not big. Shrimp are shrimps! Not even a "jumbo" shrimp is big, compared with an adult American lobster.

Most shrimp are less than 8 inches (20 centimeters) long. In addition to their size differences, shrimp and lobster also have different modes of locomotion. Lobsters usually crawl. Most shrimp are swimmers.

Many shrimp differ from lobsters in yet another way. Female lobsters carry their eggs. Many large shrimp do not. Instead, female shrimp release their eggs in the sea.

There are also freshwater shrimp, but no freshwater lobsters. Fairy shrimp, which swim continuously on their backs, are an example of freshwater shrimp.

Fairy shrimp

# Do All Crustaceans Live in Water?

Most crustaceans live in water. However, there are a few crustaceans that are completely adapted to terrestrial, or land, life. The wood louse, also called the sow bug or the pill bug, is one of these unusual crustaceans. It lives its whole life on land. Although it may look very much like a bug, it is actually a crustacean.

You may be able to find wood lice in your backyard, patio, schoolyard, or local park. Wood lice may live in rotting logs, under the bark of trees, under flowerpots, or beneath thick piles of leaves. Wood lice are almost always found in damp places, though there are a few species of desert wood lice.

When a wood louse is touched, it curls into a small ball like a miniature armadillo.

Wood lice

# Which Is the Smallest Crustacean?

Water fleas make up a group of tiny animals. They mostly live in freshwater ponds and lakes, but a few species live in the ocean. Water fleas can be as tiny as $\frac{1}{125}$ inch (0.2 millimeter) long. Larger species can grow to be as long as $\frac{3}{4}$ inch (18 millimeters), which is still very small.

Water fleas have a see-through shell. If a water flea is big enough, you can look through its shell to see its heart pumping and its other organs working.

Water fleas are not really fleas, they are crustaceans. But they look as if they are hopping through the water, as fleas hop on land, and that is probably how they got their name.

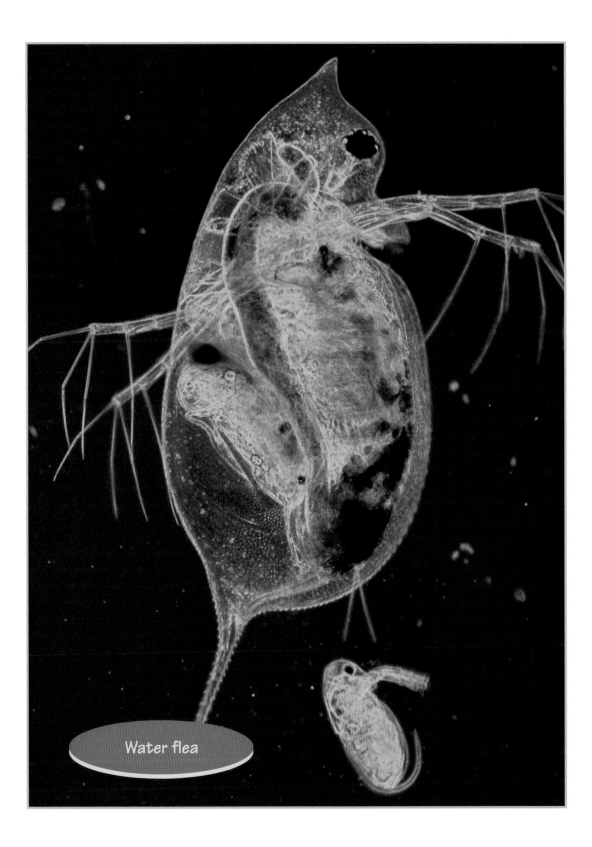

Water flea

# Are Horseshoe Crabs Crustaceans?

They have a hard, wide shell. They live on the seabed. And their name includes the word "crab." But horseshoe crabs are neither crustaceans nor crabs. They actually are more closely related to scorpions and spiders.

Several differences separate the horseshoe crab from true crabs. True crabs have antennae, but horseshoe crabs do not. True crabs have 8 walking legs, plus 2 claws, whereas, horseshoe crabs have 10 walking legs.

Horseshoe crabs are not, however, totally unrelated to crabs. Scientists classify such crustaceans as true crabs, as well as horseshoe crabs, into a larger group of animals known as Arthropoda. Arthropods are animals with jointed legs, an exoskeleton made of chitin, and bodies that are divided into sections. Insects, crustaceans, spiders, and horseshoe crabs are all arthropods. In fact, about two-thirds of all the species of animals on the planet are arthropods.

Horseshoe crabs

# Can Crabs Swim?

Most crabs walk sideways underwater on their eight legs. There are, however, some crabs that also can swim.

The blue crab is a swimming crab. To help it swim, it has modified legs. Its two hind legs are flattened at the end like a pair of oars. Blue crabs swim by "rowing" with these oarlike legs. Even though blue crabs can swim, they do not usually swim straight forward. They swim like they walk … sideways!

The scientific name for the blue crab is *Callinectes sapidus*. *Callinectes* is Latin for "beautiful swimmer." Blue crabs have brilliant blue markings on their legs and shell. Sometimes they look like they have been dipped in blue paint. Blue crabs are found on the Atlantic coast of the United States.

Blue crab

49

# Which Crabs Climb Trees?

Several species of crab, called mangrove crabs, or tree crabs, can climb well. These crabs live in mangrove forests, where mangrove trees rise out of warm coastal waters like ladders. The crabs climb these trees to search for food.

During the sizzling heat of the day, the crabs cool off on tree trunks, near the waterline. At dusk, they begin crawling up the trees to feed on algae and on plant material, including leaves. By late at night, tree trunks and branches can be covered with tree-climbing crabs.

Many types of crab beside mangrove crabs spend a lot of time on land. The ghost crab is an example. It scampers across sandy beaches looking for dinner. Coconut crabs are another land-living crab. Their favorite food is coconut. They break open the coconut shells with their strong front claws.

These and most other crabs, however, must reproduce in water. Nearly all crabs spend their early life stages as swimming larvae.

Mangrove crab

# What's Special About a Barnacle?

Adult barnacles attach themselves to rocks and other hard surfaces. They feed on living things, or organisms *(AWR guh nihz uhmz)*, that float in the water. Barnacles have special limbs or body parts that gather these organisms in so that the barnacle can feed on them. Because barnacles are attached to, and rarely move from, their perches, they have developed a special way to produce young without any mate.

A barnacle is called a hermaphrodite *(hur MAF ruh dyt)*. That means that barnacles have both male and female reproductive organs. They can produce both sperm (male reproductive cells) and eggs (female reproductive cells).

This reproductive strategy allows them to fertilize themselves and produce offspring, even when there are no other barnacles nearby. If two barnacles happen to be close to one another, however, they can mate and produce young.

Gooseneck barnacle

# How Do Fiddler Crabs Change Throughout the Day?

Fiddler crabs change by turning the color of their shell light during the day and dark at night.

Fiddler crabs are small tropical crabs that burrow in mud and sand along seacoasts. They leave their burrows and scamper across beaches and underwater in search of food. At night, when the tide has receded and they are on land, the crabs are dark. In daytime, the tide has covered them again, and they are light colored. Scientists think that the crabs have evolved this ability to change to be less visible to predators.

Amazingly, fiddler crabs kept in total darkness continue to darken and lighten based upon the time of day. How? A fiddler crab has an internal biological clock, which marks the passage of time, even in the absence of such cues as sunlight. (Humans also have biological rhythms, which can influence moods and sleep patterns.)

Fiddler crab

# Which Crab Carries Its Home on Its Back?

A hermit crab is a crab that does not have its own hard shell. A hermit crab carries a discarded snail shell on its back for protection.

A hermit crab's soft body is naturally flexible and can twist easily to fit into the spiral interior of a snail's shell. As a hermit crab becomes bigger, it outgrows its shell and shops for another.

Sometimes, hermit crabs carry other organisms, such as sea anemones, on their shells. These hitchhikers help camouflage the crabs. When a hermit crab changes shells, often the anemone will transfer to the new shell and continue along with its crab friend.

In places where discarded shells are hard to come by, hermit crabs may cover themselves with pieces of bamboo or coconut shell. Others hide among coral reefs.

Hermit crab next to its empty shell

# Which Is the Most Common Type of Crustacean?

Crustaceans called copepods are the most abundant of all the crustaceans. Some scientists believe that copepods are the most numerous multicellular animals (animals with more than one cell) found in water. Most copepods are about $\frac{1}{17}$ inch (1.5 millimeters) long.

Copepods are part of the plankton *(PLANGK tuhn)*, a large variety of tiny organisms, that float or swim near the water's surface. They live in both fresh and saltwater. Copepods feed on other, smaller members of the plankton. In turn, other animals, especially small fish, eat copepods. The protein that copepods supply to the other animals that feed upon them is an important part of the aquatic food chain.

Not all copepods are free swimmers. Many are parasites *(PAR uh sytz)*, which are organisms that live and feed on other animals. Parasitic copepods infect the skin, gills, mouth, and eyes of fish.

Copepod

# Are Crustaceans in Danger?

Most crustaceans are not in danger. Most crustaceans are so small, numerous, and widely distributed that scientists are not concerned for their survival. There are plenty of most types of these small animals.

Crustaceans harvested for human consumption are a different story. However, commercial fishers, marine biologists, and environmentalists often disagree about the status of species that are harvested commercially for human consumption. They disagree about the reasons for the decline of these species in the wild.

One thing is certain, however—things have changed in the sea. The giant American lobsters that once were found in the waters of the Atlantic coast of the United States are no longer seen. The average size of a lobster caught today is about 1 pound (0.45 kilogram). In the past, 20-, 30-, and 40-pound (9-, 14-, and 18-kilogram) lobsters were common.

American lobster

# Crustacean Fun Facts

→ The largest kind of crustacean, the giant spider crab of Japan, measures up to 12 feet (3.7 meters) across between its outstretched claws. The smallest crustaceans, such as water fleas, can be smaller than $\frac{1}{125}$ inch (0.2 millimeter) long.

→ Lobsters have teethlike structures in their stomach, which grind partially digested food. The structure is called a gastric mill.

→ Why are they called fiddler crabs? Male fiddler crabs have one large claw, which they wave in the air to impress females and intimidate other males. If you use some imagination, it looks like the male is playing a fiddle, or violin.

→ Some species of shrimp are luminescent *(LOO muh NEHS uhnt)*, meaning they produce a faint light.

→ Soft-shelled crabs are blue crabs that have just molted their shells.

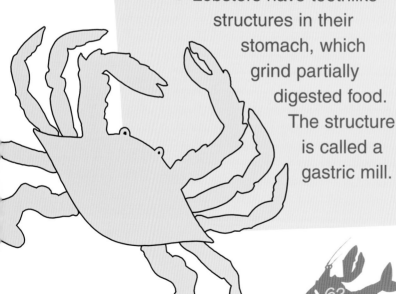

# Glossary

**arthropod**  Member of a large group of animals that includes insects and crustaceans; arthropods have jointed legs and hard outer skeletons.

**biological clock**  A built-in body system that helps animals keep track of time.

**carapace**  A shell or bony part covering a crustacean's back.

**carrion**  The flesh of dead animals that is eaten by other animals.

**chitin**  The material that makes up the shells of arthropods.

**compound eye**  An eye that is made up of many tiny lenses.

**copepod**  A tiny crustacean that is eaten by fish and some other water animals.

**crustacean**  Any of various arthropods that usually live in the water, such as lobsters, crabs, and shrimp.

**exoskeleton**  The hard outer shell that covers and protects the bodies of arthropods.

**gill**  A feathery, blood-filled organ that some animals use to take in oxygen from the surrounding water.

**hermaphrodite**  An animal with both male and female reproductive organs.

**invertebrate**  An animal that does not have a backbone.

**krill**  Small crustaceans that make up the main food for many whales and penguins.

**larva**  A young form of an animal that looks very different from the adult animal.

**molting**  The process in which an arthropod sheds its old shell and replaces it with a larger shell.

**plankton**  Tiny organisms that float or swim near the water's surface.

**regeneration**  The process in which an animal can grow a new limb to replace a lost limb.

**swimmeret**  Leglike body part that a lobster uses for swimming.

# Index

(**Boldface** indicates a photo or illustration.)

**For more information about Lobsters and Other Crustaceans, try these resources:**

*About Crustaceans*, by Cathryn Sill, Peachtree Publishers, 2004.

*Crabs, Lobsters, and Shrimps*, by Allison Lassieur, Franklin Watts, 2003.

*Pill Bugs and Sow Bugs and Other Crustaceans*, by Elaine Pascoe, Blackbirch Press, 2001.

http://www.bigelow.org/hatch_to_catch/

http://octopus.gma.org/lobsters/index.html

http://ourworld.compuserve.com/homepages/BMLSS/Hermits.htm

http://www.vims.edu/adv/ed/crab/

# Crustacean Classification

Scientists classify animals by placing them into groups. The animal kingdom is a group that contains all the world's animals. Phylum, class, order, and family are smaller groups. Each phylum contains many classes. A class contains orders, an order contains families, and a family contains individual species. Each species also has its own scientific name. Here is how the animals in this book fit into this system.

## Crustaceans and their relatives (Phylum Arthropoda)

### Subphylum Chelicerata
#### Horseshoe crabs (Class Merostomata)

### Subphylum Crustacea
#### Barnacles and copepods (Class Maxillopoda)

#### Branchiopods (Class Branchiopoda)

##### Water flea (Order Cladocera)

##### Fairy Shrimp  (Order Anostraca)

#### Lobsters and their relatives (Class Malacostraca)

##### Krill (Order Eucarida)

##### Lobsters, Crabs, Crayfishes, and Shrimps (Order Decapoda)

**Blue crab and its relatives (Family Portunidae)**
Blue crab . . . . . . . . . . . . . . . . . . . . . . . . . . . . . . . . . . . . .*Callinectes sapidus*

**Clawed lobster (Family Nephropidae)**
American lobster . . . . . . . . . . . . . . . . . . . . . . . . . . . . . . .*Homarus americanus*

**Coconut crab and its relatives (Family Coenobitidae)**
**Crayfish (Family Cambaridae)**
**Deep-sea lobster (Family Polychelidae)**
**Fiddler and ghost crab (Family Ocypodidae)**
Ghost crab . . . . . . . . . . . . . . . . . . . . . . . . . . . . . . . . . . . . .*Ocypode quadrata*

**Hermit Crab (Family Paguridae)**
**Mangrove Crab and their relatives (Family Sesarmidae)**
**Slipper Lobster (Family Scyllaridae)**
**Spider Crab (Family Majidae)**
Japanese spider crab . . . . . . . . . . . . . . . . . . . . . . . . . . . .*Macrocheira kaempferi*

**Soldier crab (Family Mictyridae)**
Soldier crab . . . . . . . . . . . . . . . . . . . . . . . . . . . . . . . . . . . .*Mictyris longicarpus*

**Spiny lobster (Family Palinuridae)**
**Stone crayfish (Family Astacidae)**

#### Wood lice and their relatives (Order Isopoda)